Survival Guide for People Facing Domestic Violence Charges in Los Angeles

AF881334

Ronald D. Hedding

Speakeasy Publishing
73-03 Bell Blvd, #10
Oakland Gardens, NY 11364
www.speakeasypublishinginc.com

Ordering Information:

Quantity sales. Special discounts are available on quantity purchases by corporations, associations, and others. For details, contact the publisher at the address above.

Orders by U.S. trade bookstores and wholesalers. Please contact Speakeasy Publishing: Tel: (888) 991-2766 or visit www.speakeasypublishinginc.com.

Printed in the United States of America.

Published in 2019.

ISBN: 978-1-946481-82-5

PREFACE

If you find yourself on the wrong end of the law related to a domestic violence charge or if you are a significant other looking for answers for your loved one, I sympathize with you. I wrote this book as a stepping stone to getting answers and taking control back of your life.

When it comes to being arrested, having to post a bail to get out of jail, and facing criminal charges, it is no joke. You quickly realize what is at stake and it is crucial to find someone who has successfully been down the road you are about to travel to guide you through the process.

Over the past 25 years, I have stared into the eyes of many clients and the families of those clients, as we sit down to strategize the best moves to make in a domestic violence situation. We must decide the best course for what can be a sometimes murky and scary future. I believe that leveling with the client and their family is the best practice. I let them know what they are truly up against; not some sugar coated version.

It is with an iron will that we must forge ahead to meet the unknown and come out the other end better, smarter, and with a game plan to get you out of the criminal justice system as quickly and as unscathed as possible. I am well prepared and battle tested, when it comes to doing what is necessary to obtain the result that you must have.

DEDICATION

This book is dedicated to those people who are able to survive a domestic violence charge in Los Angeles County and come out the other end with a new lease on life. It is not easy to survive a domestic violence charge and it will take work, perseverance, and skill to deal with your case and be a better person for it.

I'm here to tell you that you can survive the criminal justice system and learn from the mistakes that put you in this position. I have handled thousands of domestic violence cases and have seen success in action. It starts with a game plan and a realistic look at your case and what it will take to get the result you deserve.

Not every case is treated the same and there is no cookie cutter approach. You have a lot on the line and it will take a strategy that makes sense for your circumstance in order to win. The first step is picking up the phone and moving the case one step closer to being resolved the right way with the best result.

DISCLAIMER

This publication is intended to be used for educational purposes only. No legal advice is being given, and no attorney-client relationship is intended to be created by reading this material. The author assumes no liability for any errors or omissions or for how this book or its contents are used or interpreted, or for any consequences resulting directly or indirectly from the use of this book. For legal or any other advice, please consult an experienced attorney or the appropriate expert, who is aware of the specific facts of your case and is knowledgeable in the law in your jurisdiction.

Hedding Law Firm

Los Angeles Criminal Defenders

(866) 986-2092

www.la-criminaldefense.com

TESTIMONIALS

"Mr. Ronald Hedding is amazing, handling my case superbly! I had a domestic violence case and I was panicked as hell. Mr. Ron Hedding listened to me very patiently, asked many questions and took all of my concerns seriously. He walked me through possible outcomes and what he could do to help me. Without any hesitation, I chose him as my attorney, after consulting with several others. He was very pro-active and always kept me well informed. He had good connections in the LA court and knew the prosecutor very well. The entire hearing lasted less than 10 minutes and I walked away with the case dropped. I'm so glad that I asked him to be my attorney. I would definitely recommend him to anyone needing a criminal defense attorney. Last but not least, his price is very reasonable; the lowest among several attorneys I consulted."

— ***Ping W.***

****

"At court, Mr. Hedding Jr. instructed Martin to do everything possible to bring down the charges and they agreed. My charges were brought down from domestic violence to aggravated trespassing. Of course, my immigration lawyer was also involved, as she provided me with a letter stating how the charge of domestic violence would hurt me when reapplying for my resident card. There was good and effective communication from Martin and the DA. I was satisfied with the outcome."

— ***Diego***

****

"I was so traumatized when I was arrested for domestic violence. For me, it was a big shock because I was using self-defense, and I'd never been arrested before that. After I had an extremely bad experience with one other lawyer, I found Ronald Hedding on the AVVO website. When I met him, he was so compassionate, and he listened my story. Then, his entire team worked very seriously on my case and were so helpful to calm down my stress. I saw in court that the prosecutor really trusts Mr. Hedding. My case was totally dismissed. Ronald Daniel Hedding saved my life. I'm such so grateful to have found him."

— A Satisfied Client

****

"Mr. Hedding did a great job handling my criminal case. He was able to get the charges reduced and kept me out of jail. He is very knowledgeable and experienced. I would strongly recommend him to anyone."

— A Satisfied Client

****

"Ron is an amazing criminal defense attorney!! He's passionate about what he does, which is why he brings forth excellence!!!! Highly recommend Ron Hedding, if you need a criminal defense attorney!!!"

— Maral H.

****

TABLE OF CONTENTS

PERSONAL INTRODUCTION

Ronald D. Hedding is the founding member of the Hedding Law Firm. He has an extensive, well-rounded legal background in the area of criminal law, and has worked for the district attorney's office, a superior court judge, and as the guiding force behind the Hedding Law Firm for over 25 years. His multi-faceted experience not only sets him apart from his competitors but places him in an elite group of the best criminal defense attorneys in Southern California.

After establishing the Hedding Law Firm, Mr. Hedding dedicated himself to the pursuit of zealously defending his clients to the highest professional standards. He has traveled all over this nation, defending his clients and protecting their interests, reputations, and freedoms. It is rare to find a criminal defense attorney with the dual ability to successfully fight a case in our jury system and the uncanny skills to negotiate a favorable disposition for his clients. It is even rarer to find an attorney with the wisdom to make the appropriate decisions at the appropriate times.

Mr. Hedding has served as lead counsel in some of the most sensational criminal cases to be played out in Los Angeles Courtrooms, both at the state and federal level. He has received acclaim in newspapers, on the radio, and in national publications. The key to Mr. Hedding's success as an attorney—whether it involves a DUI or murder case—lies in his understanding of the United States criminal justice system and his clients' need to be informed of their rights and the legal options that will best serve those rights.

Current Employment Position

- Managing Attorney

Bar Admissions

- U.S. Court of Appeals, 9th Circuit
- U.S. District Court Central District of California
- Superior Court for Los Angeles County
- U.S. Supreme Court

Honors And Awards

- Criminal Defense Attorney of the Year, The Editorial Staff of Consumer Business Review, 1999

- Accepted as Life Member of the National Registry of Who's Who, 2000 - Present
- Outstanding Professional Award for Dedicated Achievements in the Field of Criminal Law - ABI - USA, 2002
- Criminal Defense Attorney of the Year - The Editorial Staff of Consumer Business Review, 2003

Professional Associations And Memberships

- San Fernando Valley Bar Association, 1994 - Present
- America Bar Association, 1995 - Present
- Association of Trial Lawyers of America, 1998 - Present
- National Association of Criminal Defense Attorneys, 1999 - Present
- California Attorneys for Criminal Justice, 1995 - Present

Experience, Credentials, And Skills

- I have been named criminal defense attorney of the year in Los Angeles.
- I have won jury trials in all of the major courthouses in Los Angeles.

- My Los Angeles-based law firm is recognized by the Bar Register of Preeminent Lawyers as being in the top five percent of criminal defense law firms in Los Angeles County.
- I have been recognized in Los Angeles magazine as part of the Super Lawyers Edition.
- I have won jury trials in Downtown Los Angeles federal courthouses.
- I have been recognized by Martindale-Hubbell as being in the top five percent of California attorneys for ethics and legal ability.
- I have volunteered for the State Bar of California as a judicial nomination commissioner. I was responsible for investigating potential judges as part of a 38-person commission. I represented Los Angeles County in the process of selecting judges for the state of California.
- The president of the United States granted a presidential pardon for one of my Los Angeles-based clients.
- I have been involved in published legal opinions related to cases I handled in Los Angeles courts.

- As a Los Angeles defense attorney, I have written articles on criminal defense subject matters in local bar publications.
- AVVO has rated me Superb 10 out of 10 for skill and legal abilities in Los Angeles courts.
- This is my fourth book on the subject of criminal defense.

CHAPTER 1

HOW DOES THE STATE OF CALIFORNIA DEFINE DOMESTIC VIOLENCE?

Over the past 25 years, the criteria for the police to arrest someone in a domestic violence scenario has expanded in many ways, especially in Los Angeles, California. Domestic violence occurs when one or both members of a domestic partnership or relationship cause physical harm to the other. The harm has to be physical. Simply yelling would not be considered domestic violence. It also has to be physical harm that is done in an unlawful manner, which means that a person who is being attacked and is exercising self-defense would not be charged with domestic violence.

Why Does It Matter Who The Aggressor Is In A Domestic Violence Case And How Do The Police Make This Determination?

It matters who the aggressor was in a domestic violence case because when both sides are physical, the aggressor will be the one who is arrested and charged with the crime.

When determining who the aggressor was in a domestic violence situation, police will be considering who caused the most damage, who is the larger party, and who won the fight. Oftentimes, these determinations are made unfairly because the police were not there and did not see what happened. When one party injures another while reasonably defending themselves, they are often arrested, which is simply not fair. In determining who the aggressor was, the police are put in a very difficult position. This is because the people involved in these situations are often emotional and manipulate the facts in order to avoid getting into trouble. It is not uncommon for the watch commander or sergeant to be called out to the scene of an incident to help determine which person was the aggressor. Even the prosecutors must sometimes second-guess the police when making their own determination as to which person was the aggressor.

Do Police In LA County Tend To Make An Arrest Regardless Of Circumstances On A Domestic Violence Call?

When the police are called to a domestic violence situation in LA County, they will usually make an arrest, unless it can be determined that no one was physically injured. If it was just a couple of people shouting at each other and a neighbor called the police, then the police probably would not make an arrest. If the police see an injury on one or both of the parties and they are unable to determine which person was the aggressor, they will just arrest both parties. This can actually work to the defense's benefit by creating a problem for the prosecutors because both parties may assert their Fifth Amendment rights, if called upon to testify. This is because when the case goes to trial or some sort of hearing and one party testifies, they may say something to incriminate themselves. If a person is charged with domestic violence in the San Fernando Valley or Los Angeles, they definitely need to obtain an attorney and be careful about what they say. In my experience, the police are not your friend and they will do everything they can to try to get you to incriminate yourself.

What Additional Charges May Accompany A Domestic Violence Arrest In LA County?

There are a number of additional charges that may accompany a domestic violence arrest in LA County. If a couple is married and living together and acts of physical force occur between them, then penal code section 273.5 would apply. Another charge I see is 243-D, which is when physical force occurs between two people who are cohabitating, such as a boyfriend and a girlfriend. I am often able to get these charges reduced to simple battery or disturbing the peace, even if the person is responsible for what they did. It will depend on what happened, how bad the injuries were, and whether or not it is difficult to determine which person was the aggressor. In most cases, there will be some sort of battery charge and the guilty party will have to take domestic violence courses, pay fines, and be on probation for three years. Depending on the gravity of what occurred, there may be other ramifications, including jail time.

CHAPTER 2

WHAT SHOULD YOU DO WHEN DOMESTIC VIOLENCE CHARGES ARE FILED AGAINST YOU?

Domestic violence charges can be very scary because, typically, the person is arrested and their liberty is taken away. This loss of control can be particularly troubling for a myriad of reasons. They have to post a $50,000 bail. Usually, the other spouse now has control of the home. If there are kids involved, a lot of times, you're prevented from seeing your kids. It really throws your world into an uproar. First and foremost, don't cause any more problems with the person claiming that you committed domestic violence against them. It will only get you deeper into trouble. You need a strategy meeting with a criminal defense attorney, who knows how to deal with domestic violence cases and is familiar with the jurisdiction where your case is pending. They'll know the prosecutors, the judges, and how these types of cases are dealt with in the court where it is pending, with your circumstances in mind.

You have to get advice from an attorney or you'll be left in the dark and have a problem getting clarity and peace of mind. Domestic violence is a very politically-charged issue and the prosecutors are used to that. Often, the alleged victim tries to change their story and the prosecution is not going to allow that to happen. They're going to call the police in and ask what they saw at the scene and what they believe. They're going to play the 9-1-1 tape, where the victim is screaming and crying. Whether people like it or not, a victim recanting doesn't solve the problem. However, it's still important to tell your attorney that your wife or husband is now on your side. That's good information to have and the attorney can figure out what, if anything, the fact that the alleged victim is no longer at odds with the defendant can accomplish.

If the judge issues a protective order which orders you not to contact the victim, then you absolutely cannot contact them. Otherwise, you're going to violate the order and you'll be looking at more criminal charges. If there's no protective order in place, then you can contact the other party, but you would only want to do that if they were amenable to that. If they're still mad at you, contacting them is probably just going to trigger more problems for you.

The best process is to get to an attorney, go over how you can beat a domestic violence charge, and let them guide you through it. If you can't beat the charges, you still want to get a strategy together as soon as possible. Once you get arrested, you can post bail and get out, and then you'll appear in court for arraignment. Your attorney will appear with you at the arraignment and the judge will issue a protective order for you to stay away from the other party while the case is pending. However, if the other party shows up and says they don't want a protective order, then the prosecutors can talk to them and decide whether or not they're going to agree to that. They may issue a modified order, allowing contact with the protected party. This type of domestic violence protective order is referred to as a level one order. The strategy on how to deal with the issuance of a criminal protective order has become more and more important in today's domestic violence defense world.

After you make your initial court appearance and your attorney is provided with all of the police reports and related evidence, the case is going to proceed and be resolved by way of a negotiated plea or go to trial, where a jury will decide whether the charged person is guilty or not guilty. There are circumstances where one spouse or party has lied and you can show the prosecutors evidence that proves this defense. If it's done sufficiently and effectively, the prosecutors can dismiss the case, if they so choose. As you may guess, this will not be easy, but can be accomplished in the right case.

Does An Alleged Victim Need To Be Injured For Domestic Violence Charges To Be Brought?

I have seen cases in which domestic violence charges were brought by a person who had no injuries but claimed that they were struck by their partner. It is much more helpful to prosecutors and law enforcement if someone has visible injuries or can otherwise prove that their partner hit them in an unlawful manner, such as with video footage. When a person claims to have been struck but has no injuries to show for it, the defense will use this evidence to their advantage in establishing credibility issues with the alleged victim. As the credibility of the alleged victim goes, so goes the prosecutor's case. The police will also have to make a judgment call as to whether or not they are actually going to make an arrest.

CHAPTER 3

STEPS TO TAKE IF YOU HAVE A DOMESTIC VIOLENCE CASE PENDING IN CRIMINAL COURT

Your first move, if you've been charged with domestic violence, should be to hire an attorney who handles domestic violence cases in the courthouse where your case is pending. Get a face to face consultation with a domestic violence lawyer in Los Angeles, CA and begin the process of defending yourself, preserving your good name, and keeping yourself out of jail! Due to the political pressures related to domestic violence cases, the police, prosecutors, and judges take a hardline in how they deal with these matters. Most of the time, they arrest the aggressor, make them post a $50,000 bail, and are tough when it comes to the terms of any proposed resolution.

The way to turn the tide in your favor is to hire a local attorney, who has defended people like you in similar situations. Hire an attorney who knows how to present your story to the players in the system who will ultimately make the decisions that dictate the impact your criminal arrest will have on your life, future, freedom, and reputation. Once your story is presented in the right way by a domestic violence attorney and any defenses you may have are asserted, you will be in a much stronger position to defend yourself and obtain a result that you can live with. Without the representation of a domestic violence lawyer in Los Angeles County by your side, this will be nearly impossible.

The judge and prosecutors have no duty to help you and their interests lie with the People of the State of California, the alleged victim, and themselves. You are last on the list and the way the system works is that your attorney is the one who will speak with you and make sure your interests are protective. This is why it is crucial that you tell you attorney the truth about what happened and let them have a good feel for what the other side will be arguing, and will be ready to counter any argument the prosecutor brings up.

CHAPTER 4

DEFENSE STRATEGIES TO USE IN DOMESTIC VIOLENCE CASES

There are many defenses that can be used in domestic violence cases but they are primarily fact-specific; your defense will be dependent on what happened in your particular case. Every fact and piece of evidence involved in the case will need to be considered before a specific defense can be formulated. Self-defense is absolutely a valid defense; if a person injures someone in the process of defending themselves from an attack, then that is not a crime. The key to self-defense, however, is that the person who was defending themselves must have used a reasonable amount of force. If someone goes too far in defending themselves, then they will be determined to be the aggressor who acted unreasonably under the circumstances, and they will be arrested and charged with domestic violence. In determining a defense, it is best to give your chosen attorney an honest account of what happened with no spin and let them help determine what the best approach should be for your particular case.

What Are The Penalties If I Am Convicted In A Domestic Violence Case?

The penalties for a domestic violence conviction depend on the severity of what occurred and the defendant's criminal record. On the low end of the scale, everyone is likely going to have to take a 52-week domestic violence course that would require them to take classes once per week for one year. In addition, almost everyone will be put on probation for three years. In LA County, there will also be a domestic violence fine. Beyond that, it is going to depend on what happened and how skilled your defense attorney is in negotiating your case and getting your story across to the powers that be.

In severe cases of domestic violence, the guilty party will face jail time and sometimes even prison. If it is filed as a misdemeanor, then they could serve up to a year in the county jail. If it is filed as a felony, then they could serve up to six years in prison. Depending on the severity of injuries, the jail sentence could be even longer. There are a whole host of other penalties available to the prosecutor and judge, depending on what they believe is appropriate and whether your attorney can convince them of your position.

If, for example, alcohol was involved in the incident, then the person will have to attend AA meetings and perform community service. Anger management courses can also be imposed by the judge. It depends on what happened and what the prosecutors feel will get the person in line, so that they do not do anything else to their spouse or significant other.

Losing Your Gun Rights Related To A Domestic Violence Charge

Domestic violence charges are particularly politically charged, as it relates to certain rights. We have the right to bear arms but if you are convicted of a domestic violence related charge, you will lose that right for at least ten years.

This seems unfair to a lot of people, but it is the legislature's way of trying to protect victims of domestic violence and they feel as though anyone who takes things to the level of injuring their spouse or loved one should not have the ability to bear arms and potentially act in a more dangerous manner.

Potentially Reducing Charges To A Lesser Offense

A lot of times in domestic violence cases, if the person has no criminal record and it's not a situation where there's a severe injury, we can get their domestic violence charges reduced to simple battery, disturbing the peace, trespassing, or a host of other lesser included misdemeanor charges. However, you still lose your ability to bear arms, if you get convicted of one of these charges. The prosecutors do not like to reduce charges, especially in domestic violence related cases. It will take a skilled, seasoned defense attorney, who is armed with the right information, to have a chance at success.

Is It Possible To Avoid A Criminal Conviction?

Once a domestic violence charged is filed, it is very difficult to avoid a criminal conviction. The only way you're going to get out of the weapon ban is if you don't get convicted of anything. That means your attorney either needs to convince the prosecutors to dismiss the case altogether, or you have to go to jury trial and be found not guilty. Obviously, this is no easy task, but it is possible under the right circumstances.

I recently had a case where a law enforcement officer, who got convicted of a battery, was attempting to regain his ability to own, use, and possess a weapon for work, so he wouldn't lose his employment. They've carved out an exception, as it relates to law enforcement officers; if they can show certain factors, they can use their weapon even though they have a domestic violence-related offense. For example, if someone gets a simple battery charge against a third party, having nothing to do with a spouse, that law enforcement officer is going to lose their ability to own, use, or possess a weapon. Therefore, they'll probably lose their job as well.

The reason they've carved out this domestic violence exception for law enforcement officers who are convicted of spousal abuse charges is because they want to still allow those officers to work, under certain circumstances, as the victim/spouse is going to end up losing income as well, if their spouse loses their career. Sometimes, the domestic violence law looks to help those offenders who need certain accommodations, while other times, the legislature and court system simply do not care and value the protection of society over that of a person who has violated the law.

CHAPTER 5

HOW MUCH WOULD IT COST TO POST BAIL IN A DOMESTIC VIOLENCE RELATED ARREST?

In a typical domestic violence case, bail is set at around $50,000, which is quite high. The bond companies usually want some sort of collateral and are going to charge anywhere from seven to 10 percent for the premium. Everyone is entitled to a bail, but if it is a weekend or a holiday, the person could sit in jail for several days until there is a bail commissioner available and until they can request a release on their own recognizance. If the bail commissioner lets the person out before the arraignment, then they would not have to pay anything, as long as they promise to appear in court. If someone waits until they get to court and their attorney argues for a bail, there is a chance to save significant money on bail. It is my experience that most people will bail out at the first available opportunity because they can't stand being in custody.

For weak cases in which there were not many injuries and it is difficult to determine which person was the aggressor, the bail might be set at $20,000. In many cases, the police seem to realize that people are emotional, perhaps drunk, and involved in a volatile situation. As a solution, the police will take one of the individuals away in order to prevent the situation from escalating. There have been cases all over LA County in which the police, prosecutors, or judges could have prevented one spouse from ultimately killing the other by simply taking one spouse into custody before things escalated to that point. This is what the police really want to prevent; it is their goal to protect both parties and if that means that they need to arrest someone in order to keep two people separated, then that is what they'll do. In fact, if the police came to a location where there has been a physical altercation, it is there policy to arrest whomever they determine is the aggressor.

CHAPTER 6

WHEN IS A RESTRAINING ORDER OR AN ORDER OF PROTECTION PUT IN PLACE?

Between the arrest and the first court appearance, the victim in a domestic violence case can seek and obtain a restraining order. Once the prosecutor files a domestic violence charge and the person makes their first court appearance, the judge and prosecutor will put a protective order in place. When a person is being charged with a misdemeanor, any attorney could technically appear for them but in domestic violence cases, the defendant must appear at the first court appearance, so the court can put a criminal protective order in place. This is because a protective order will be issued and the receiver of that order must be present. Additionally, that person must be told by the judge that they are not allowed to go near their significant other. If the significant other shows up at the arraignment and tells the prosecutor that they do not want a protective order, depending on how dangerous the other party is, the prosecutors will usually issue a level one protective order. More and more the prosecutors and judges will not let the parties in a domestic violence case see each other during the pendency of the criminal case and until they feel the situation is safe.

Can I Be In Contact With My Kids When Facing A Domestic Violence Charge In LA County?

If someone has a domestic violence charge in LA County, they will typically be allowed to see their children. The issue revolves around the facilitation of those visits. If a defendant's significant other has custody of the kids and there is a protective order related to them, then that is going to make it difficult for the defendant to see their kids. Under such circumstances, a third party may need to be utilized. However, involving third parties can become dangerous because the other person could lie or seek a protective or restraining order that covers themselves and the children. If that becomes the case and the defendant wants to pursue a divorce, then they would need to retain an attorney in order to gain some level of custody over the children. Alternatively, a level one protective order could be requested, which is a peaceful protective order that allows a person to see their spouse and children while the case is pending. This is something to discuss with your attorney at the initial meeting with them.

CHAPTER 7

CAN PROSECUTORS PROVE A DOMESTIC VIOLENCE CASE IF THE VICTIM DOESN'T WANT TO TESTIFY?

I frequently have clients calling me, saying that their significant other is not going to cooperate with their domestic violence case. The victim is not going to testify, therefore, they think they're going to automatically win the case. Unfortunately, this is not true. There are a lot of different ways the prosecutors can go when it comes to cases where individuals have a change of heart and do not want their significant other prosecuted. The prosecutors can't tell whether someone who is recanting is actually recanting in a sincere manner or not. They are used to recanting witnesses in domestic violence cases and have strategies to deal with his situation.

Prosecutors Will Seek Justice And Punishment

Prosecutors only care about justice and punishing those individuals who they perceive were involved in domestic violence-related actions toward another person.

They have special units that only handle domestic violence-related offenses and they have orders in Los Angeles County to make sure that offenders are punished, lose their gun rights, have a protective order put in place, serve jail time, and complete domestic violence classes.

The other party choosing not to testify is not going to stop them. They're going to try to find that party and serve a subpoena on them. If that party gets on the witness stand and says that they don't want to testify, the judge is going to order them to testify anyway. Once they get them on the witness stand, they will bring up the statement they gave to the police at the scene of the incident. If there were any injuries involved, they're going to be able to make a run at getting a conviction in the case. If the alleged victim changes their story, the prosecutor will call the original police officers who took statements at the scene to make their case. In today's criminal defense world, many times, the alleged victim's statement is memorialized on a body cam video.

Admission Of Hearsay Statements

There is always the possibility that the victim doesn't show up to court. In some circumstances, even if the alleged victim doesn't show up, the prosecutors can still get their statement in. An excited utterance is an exception to the hearsay rule. I've also had cases where they've gotten the victim or the defendant's statement on body-worn camera video by the Los Angeles police department. The 9-1-1 call can be used. This is powerful evidence that can be used at a trial, even if the person is not there. Lastly, there is case law which allows statements to come in under certain circumstances. even if the alleged victim doesn't show up to the trial.

The Victim Can't Drop The Charges

Just because your significant other wants to take back everything they said in the heat of the moment does not mean that the prosecutors will dismiss your case. The case will have to be resolved in another way. How a domestic violence case is dealt with in Los Angeles County depends on the posture of the case and the strength of the prosecution's evidence. If there are no injuries on the alleged victim, their story does not make sense, and they are not willing to cooperate with the prosecutors, it will be difficult for the government to get a conviction. Your best defense will almost always be one that you and your attorney have planned out, based on the facts and circumstances surrounding your case.

When I meet with clients, I like to get all of the facts out on the table. This includes the good, the bad, and the ugly of what happened. Putting a spin on things really doesn't do you any good. I need the details of what happened and I need them from the police's perspective, so I can assess if we can effectively counter them. Only giving me your side of the story ends up leaving important pieces of the puzzle out of the equation and it is difficult to truly craft a solution. Once we have everything out related to the incident, then we can set about figuring out what needs to be done to achieve the best result in your case. We must have an honest conversation and then, I can use my years of experience to assist in figuring out the right moves to make.

Without a game plan in a domestic violence case, your chances of achieving a successful outcome decrease dramatically and your fate will be left up to luck and the whim of the judge and prosecutor in the court where your case is pending. This is not a recipe for achieving the best result. You must join forces with your chosen attorney, as your first step to success. You and your attorney can then begin the process of shaping your destiny as it relates to your domestic violence case.

CHAPTER 8

DOMESTIC VIOLENCE: A CASE STUDY IN LOS ANGELES COUNTY

There is a case called *Crawford,* which allows the prosecution to admit certain hearsay evidence, even though the victim in a domestic violence case is not available. I had a case recently where that's exactly what the prosecutors did. They filed a motion with the judge to bring in the alleged victim's statement through the police officers who took the initial police report. They had a 9-1-1 tape of the alleged victim saying a lot of incriminating information about my client and they had my client's statement to the police. In addition to that 9-1-1 tape, they called the police officers to testify how the wife looked when they got there and how the inside of the house looked. They were trying to support that 9-1-1 tape, which basically said my client had punched his wife in the face.

After they were done, we called my client to the witness stand and he gave his version of the events. Fortunately for us, he was a large man and a punch to the face really wasn't substantiated because the wife had no injury to her face. It didn't make any sense to the jury. We also ended up tracking down the wife and calling her as a witness. She gave her account and indicated that she didn't tell the truth about everything that happened, and explained why. We were able to get a not guilty verdict in the case.

This is an example of how some domestic violence cases in Los Angeles County can take strange turns. It is unfair, in my opinion, that this *Crawford* case allows the prosecution to put on certain evidence and then, the defense doesn't have an opportunity to cross-examine and confront that evidence. How is the defense supposed to cross-examine or defend against a 9-1-1 tape? We can't ask the person because they're not there. Now, the police are using *Crawford* to get in domestic violence witness statements when the police come and they have a body camera on. That body camera evidence can be used in domestic violence or spousal abuse cases in Los Angeles, even if the alleged victim is nowhere to be found at the time of trial. How is the defense supposed to cross-examine that person? If there are inconsistencies in their story, how is the defense supposed to point those inconsistencies out and challenge the alleged victim on them?

The best evidence in these cases is to be able to cross-examine the alleged victim and ask them, for example, if it is true that they were punched in the face by a 225-pound man and if so, how there is no injury. The answer to that question will destroy the case for the prosecutor because it's going to be clear that the person did not tell the truth. If you have a domestic violence case in LA County, it's time to stand up for yourself and make the moves necessary to protect you rights. Get on the phone with an attorney now. Even if there's no defense in the case, you must do everything in your power to mitigate the situation and do damage control right from the beginning.

WHAT IS THE NEXT STEP?

Pick up the phone and set up a face to face consultation with me and we can begin the process of taking control of your case and your fate! Just burying your head in the sand and hoping for the best is going to lead to disaster.

In today's domestic violence world, you must be proactive about how you treat your case. At your first court appearance, in most cases, the prosecutor is going to ask that you stay 100 yards away from the other party, as of the day of the court appearance. This means that if you live with the other party, you have to move out, whether they want you to or not.

This is only the tip of the iceberg headed your way, as it relates to some of the potential consequences associated with any type of domestic violence prosecution. You must figure out what you are up against and begin the process of taking control of your case back, and taking back control of your own destiny! We are here to help.

INDEX

S

T

NOTES

Made in the USA
Monee, IL
05 November 2026

67385064R00031